THE

SILVER

LINING

A Little Faith Is All It Takes

BY: NATALIE N. DIXON

NATALIE N. DIXON
ISBN—13: 978—0615775074
ISBN—10: 0615775071

Author:
Natalie N. Dixon

Cover Design by:
Natalie N. Dixon
&
TLF PUBLISHING GROUP

Manufactured in the United States of America

Author

Natalie Dixon

Natalie Dixon is a 36 year old mother of 5 children, 3 boys and 2 girls.

She lives in Kansas

I have always loved to pour my emotions into poetry since I was a young girl. Writing has always been a part of who I am, although outside of family, I really never shared it.

I began really putting my time into writing again after my mother passed in April 07 to help deal with the pain. I than started sharing my breakthrough online at the end of 2010 and seen the effect my poetry has had on so many people. Which has encouraged me to take it to the next level, and here we are.

My favorite style of writing is inspirational and motivational poetry. I also write lyrics, short stories, and erotica.

ACKNOWLEDGEMENTS

First, I have to give all glory to God. Without him, I would still be a broken soul, lost, and without a voice. The very reason why I am dedicating my first book to share some of my beliefs based off my life and what the Lord has done for me.

To my kids, seems like we wouldn't make it through some of the trials we have faced together as a family, but we did, and we will continue to. Je'vaughn, Lavon'te, De'Naje, De'Ayla, and Ci're, you are my motivation and always have been.

To my family, R.I.P. mama, My brothers Albert and Sedrick Whitaker, I love each and every one of you, and I thank those of you that never let me fall. Especially my cousin Janine Francois, and my lifelong friends Tawanna and Charity Smith.

Outside of the family I grew up with, I am blessed to have found a group of friends that I write with online and can relate to like a family. I have learned so much through our friendships. There's far too many to name, I'm positive they know who they are though. To name a few there's Lakeita Johnson, my Godmother, O' how I love you so. My personal guardian angel, and there's no other description that fits you.

Bernard Washington, aka Knowledge, you have kept me stable so many times and have shown me so much love. Love you. Lynnett Fox. aka Ms.FOxxxy, we may not be blood, but you already know we are connected for life. We have been tried and proved to be true. Love ya

THE SILVER LINING

To all my Diva Sisters, past and present, as well as my Kommission brothers, I truly love and appreciate you all so much. You all have helped me in more ways than you may ever know.

To Antonio Moore aka Reloaded and my brother Daimian E. aka Theghost02, You know what? You two are some true riders and was down for me no matter what, whenever. Much love always.

To The Lyricist Firm Family, Mike Sudler aka Brooklyn, We started at the bottom together, and here we are now. Steadily climbing! One Family··· One Love! E'Nuff said!

To the R.I.C.H. Familia, You were there for me and encouraged me at a time when I was still kind of unsure of my talent and helped me to break out of my shell. I will never forget and will always respect that.

May God Continue to Bless us all . XOXO

Natalie Dixon

THE SILVER LINING

TABLE OF CONTENTS

1.	The Silver Lining	Page 1
2.	The Concrete Rose	Page 2
3.	The Best Things In Life Are Free	Page 4
4.	Diosa (Goddess)	Page 7
5.	Today We Thank You O'Lord	Page 9
6.	A Brand New Me	Page 12
7.	No More Pain	Page 13
8.	I Will Survive	Page 15
9.	The Stories We Tell	Page 17
10.	Signs Of Fire	Page 19
11.	Tonight's Storm	Page 22
12.	Back To Basics	Page 26
13.	The Wayward Soul	Page 28
14.	Less And Less	Page 34
15.	Today's Prayer	page 36
16.	Willing To Fight	Page 38
17.	Reality Check	Page 40
18.	That's A Fact	Page 42
19.	Beauty Is	Page 44
20.	No Doubt	Page 46
21.	Judgment Day	Page 47
22.	Predestined Steps	Page 48
23.	Pushing Positivity	Page 50
24.	Where Is The Love	Page 51
25.	All Of Our Strength	Page 54
26.	Humanity's War	Page 56
27.	Born To Be Free	Page 59
28.	The Caretaker	Page 62
29.	My Reflections	Page 64
30.	I Know Of A Place	Page 67
31.	Picked From The Garden	Page 70
32.	Generations	Page 73
33.	Say What You Mean, Mean What You Say	Page 78
34.	That Little Girl	Page 80
35.	Live And Learn	Page 83

36.	Self-Destruction	Page 85
37.	Love, Compassion, And Forgiveness	Page 86
38.	The Storm Chasers	Page 88
39.	Jesus Take The Lead	Page 90
40.	Trick Or Treat	Page 93
41.	His Creation	Page 96
42.	No Guarantees	Page 97
43.	Just Wait	Page 99
44.	Stronger Than Ever	Page 101
45.	The Broken Soul	Page 102
46.	Heaven Is My Fate	Page 104
47.	Final Destination	Page 106
48.	Footprints In The Sand	Page 108
49.	From The Cradle To The Grave	Page 109
50.	Wait Till Your Father Comes Home	Page 113
51.	A Little Faith	Page 117
52.	A Woman's Worth	Page 120
53.	A Woman Scorned	Page 122
54.	The Absence Of Purpose	Page 125
55.	The Devil Is A Lie	Page 127
56.	Back On Track	Page 129

The Silver Lining

Behind a sky full of storm clouds
the sun is patiently waiting to come out and
shine
Darkness takes over and blackens the nights,
but the morning hours will never fail to
bring us back the light.
GOD has complete control, and he proves it
with all his complex designs.
So I leave my life in his hands as well,
trusting that even when situations aren't
looking fine, in the end, everything will be
alright.
The security I find in Jesus has given me
hope on restless nights.
With faith, I can still find many reasons to
smile instead of cry.
I just had to stop allowing negative thoughts
to consume my mind.
And learn how to focus on the beauty of the
silver lining from time to time.

THE CONCRETE ROSE

*She lived her life standing all alone
surrounded by weeds and hay
on a lonely country road*

*She's been holding her ground
unsheltered ,
through many many storms*

*But , she was growing tired
and her spirit was broke.*

*Throughout time her petals
had become withered and slightly torn...*

*She couldn't bare the pain
of the rough winds anymore.*

So one day she looked upon the Lord

*First, thanking him for all he's done
for supplying the rain and the sun*

Which kept her alive and helped her grow...

*Now the seasons are changing
and winter is about to approach.*

*She feared being suffocated
to death by the snow*

*there's no help for me Lord,
she cried out, once I'm exposed to the cold.*

*I will crack and fall into pieces
once my exterior is froze...*

THE SILVER LINING

Just then, she felt his presence,
and from behind an old oak tree that was close,
a magnificent and holy image arose...

She instantly felt a sense of warmth,
peace and hope

A mighty voice greeted her n said hello

Shed was speechless
and attracted by the image and how it glowed...

Be calm ,
your faith in me has lead me to you
explained the Lord

Than out of nowhere a stream appeared
And surrounded her as it began to flow

the thick substance formed a shell ,

preserving her beauty,
covering every petal and every thorn.
Her very essence had been captured
within the strength of the hardened stone.

And that was the beginning of what is known as...

THE CONCRETE ROSE

THE BEST THINGS IN LIFE ARE FREE

It seems as if the best things in life are free

so why do we put so much value on materialistic things?

There's no price that we owe on the gift of life

or the air that we so freely breathe.

Our salvation

been paid for by our Father

so that too, was just giving unto thee.

Wisdom and knowledge are

gained through experience,

and no amount of money can purchase

the mindset those qualities bring

Love...

The strongest emotion in the world and it doesn't cost a thing

An act of kindness

priceless

but a blessing to the one who had received.

Unity...

when two or more gather for whatever it is that they may believe

all I know is the bond between them doesn't cost a thing...

THE SILVER LINING

Why can't we stay focused on the truth

instead of allowing ourselves to be trained by society...

All things on earth will be left on earth

when the Lord returns, and we leave

money, cars n homes is needed

True.

But I will never allow those things to justify me.

I am rich enough in blessings

and that's more than enough for me.

I'd give up the shirt off my back,

or my last meal

to someone who's in need.

Yet, so many people get caught up

and controlled by the spirit of greed.

People say money rules the world,

but the world was created with love,

so I find that hard to believe.

From what I see,

the only things really worth having

are and will always be free.

DIOSA
(Goddess)

Born unto the world as an innocent baby girl,
not knowing what we have yet to face.
Created out of love,
and blessed with beauty,
strength, compassion, dignity, and grace.
Knowledge, experience and wisdom,
doesn't come easy.
Those are qualities that through life,
are eventually gained.
Unless you let yourself get stuck
instead of dusting yourself off
and getting back into the race.
It took a long time for me to look inside,
and find the true me.
Yet, if I was able go back in time,
I wouldn't change a thing.

Today I am

A PHENOMINAL WOMAN,

A MOTHER,
A LOVER,
A GODDESS,
A QUEEN.

Once we as woman realize how powerful we are
"our self-worth." There's nothing that will ever be
allowed to stand in our way.
We spend so much time trying to survive,
thrive and protect what's ours,
so we naturally learn to be territorial
of who is in our space.

Silent and observant
but loud and clear when it's time for us
to step up to the plate.

To obe the voice of reason
when confusion and chaos comes into play.
Where there's a need for a healing touch
it is there, our nurturing hands will lay.

To produce and water heavens seeds
by making sure we teach our children the
importance of following the commandments
that The Bible states.

TODAY WE THANK YOU O' LORD
(With KNOWLEDGE)

As we fall upon our knees to praise our God... the God of Abraham... Isaac... And Jacob...

We thank you oh Lord for the blessings which you have bestowed on us, which presently overflow our cups...

We thank you for thine 6 days you labored to create the earth on which we live.

We thank you for the mercy that you show us... Even though mercy is something we ourselves find hard to give...

We thank you for the air we breathe... As well as the warm caress we get from the sun. As we place no other before you; for regardless of the name we acknowledge you by... In our hearts we all agree that you are the one... The one who fulfilled the prophecies as Moses told Pharaoh his God said; "To let his people go". As the mighty hands of God held the Red Sea back until his people past through... Before letting it return to its natural flows... God who the pilgrims worshipped when they landed on Plymouth Rock... The same God Martin prayed to hundreds and hundreds of years after Plymouth Rock landed on us... The source of power greater than ourselves... When in our own power we cannot trust... For we know that it was only because you were carrying us.. That we only saw in our darkest hours... one set of footprints in the sand.

Then you showed your greatest gift of love when you gave your only son to atone for the sins of man...

AMEN:
Knowledge

Every day I thank you Lord, but today let me count a few of the ways...

You are more than worthy of our dedication and praise...

First off, I thank you for giving me the breath to awake and make it through another day...

I thank you for my children... Your creation that you placed under my care, to raise in your ways...

I'm thankful for your guidance... Without it, there is no telling where I would be today...

Thank you for all the reminders of the love you have for us in a world filled with so much hate...

Thank you for knowing my heart and keeping me protected from the heavy rains... For you have been here to mend the pieces each time it breaks...

Thank you for the family and friends I have been blessed with, they bring a great deal of happiness to my spirit that can't be erased...

I'm thankful that You have been patient and forgiving with me, otherwise I'd be just another sheep that has wandered astray...

Father, thank you for sacrificing your son my Lord and Savior, so I wouldn't be burdened by a life of shame...

Thank you for never giving up on me, even when the faith in myself, wasn't the same...

I thank you for the good times and the bad times... Because together they have molded me into the woman I am today.

AMEN:

Natalie Dixon

A BRAND NEW ME

RELEASED FROM CHAINS
MY PAST HAD ON ME.
FOR SO LONG
I HAVENT REALLY KNOWN
WHAT TO BELIEVE.
IRONICALLY
THE TRUTH WAS HIDDEN INSIDE
DEEP
FINALLY!
THE LORD ALLOWED ME
TO LOOK WITHIN
NOW I SEE.
WHERE I WAS STRONG
AND WHAT MADE ME WEAK
I AM THANKING YOU LORD
TODAY MY HEART FEELS FREE
BEEN SOUL SEARCHING
AND LONGING
TO EMBRACE POSITIVITY
BURDENS BEEN LIFTED
I CAN BREATHE
I WILL SUCCEED
AND IF GOD IS FOR ME
NO ONE HERE ON EARTH
CAN TAKE ANYTHING.
I PROCLAIM THAT MY BLESSINGS
WILL CONTINUE TO RAIN DOWN ON ME.
THIS IS MY REBIRTH
I AM EMBRACING THE BRAND NEW ME.

THE SILVER LINING

NO MORE PAIN

DEAR FATHER,

I know misery will be extinct
when your son return
And those without faith,
will then learn

That if we supply the faith,
then he will do the rest
Cover us and shield us,
as the devil begins his test

To weaken the bond,
between The Father and his child
To get them to lose faith in God,
so for his word we'd have denial

But how can we lose faith,
in he who created heaven and earth
Who has watched over us each day,
since our parents gave birth

At times our minds grow weak,
and we forget to let him be our guide
But still our Father is there,
right with us for the ride

THE SILVER LINING

Waiting ever so patiently,
for us to say "Father take the wheel"
That's when he'll take over,
and God will finish the deal

Don't cry no more brothers and sisters,
there's no need to live in fear
God has made a promise to us,
we have no reason for anymore tears

We ask that you guide us Lord,
in all that we do
For though there are things I can't do,
I hold all my faith in you...

I WILL SURVIVE

Love had come knocking,
but when I opened the door
it ran away.

It felt like I was so close
to a special union,
than loneliness was threw
right back in my face.

Maybe it wasn't meant to be
or maybe it just wasn't the right time.
But, I got held up trying to weigh options
and even though I wanted to,

I could never make any sense out of the lies.
There I was stuck in past time,
allowing thoughts of what could of been
to take over,
until they exhausted my mind.
I was all out of tears,
so even though my heart cried,

Sadly, no one else knew,
because my eyes remained dry.
As strong as I thought I was,
I started to lose the will to fight.

THE SILVER LINING

My voice felt restricted
I lost the desire to rhyme.
So the pain began to literally
eat me up inside.

My weakness is the need for love,
but it seems to leave me
broken every time.
It's only through Gods strength
My spirit still feels alive.

My Father never fails
to show up for me every time.
It's the small blessings
he surrounds me with daily,
that has reminded me once again

I WILL SURVIVE

THE STORIES WE TELL

If I Haven't reached the true revelation
of the tribulations I'm facing,
I'd rather keep my conversations
between God and myself.

Because, if I Haven't figured out how to overcome
my personal battles yet, How is sharing the pain
of my battle wounds going to help anyone else?

I've realized, I wasn't born to search for love
I am here to spread it, and despite what many
believe,

Real love!

My love!

Can't be found in looks or purchased with
wealth.

I've learned it will find us once we are
confident,
imperfections and all,
and can still be in love with our self.

Life isn't easy; we just have to make the best
out of whatever we are being dealt.
God never intended on us to stay down
just because we lost our balance and fell.

He walks with us, even when we are headed in
the wrong direction on the wrong trails.
We can only call a bad decision a mistake
if we have learned from the times
we have tried and failed.

Only then, others will be able to benefit from the
stories we tell.

SIGNS OF FIRE
"THE WAKE UP CALL"

We have to stop acting blind to the signs. The end is steadily moving closer in time. I pray hard for the world, not wanting to see any of us left behind. Greed rules the world today, So many rather overlook the truth, and try to justify a glamorized lie. The choices we make can be forgiven, but the damage is already in major play. As a whole, can our actions as:

Mothers,
Fathers,
Brothers.
Sisters,
and citizens···
Be justified on The Judgment Day?

The natural destructions and the enemies thirsting for our blood is only a taste of the disasters we have yet to face.

You can try to cover your secrets here on earth, but when the fire is below, and Jesus wants to know, there's nowhere to hide and no room to run away. I cling to hope and believe in faith. United I want us all, to walk through heavens gates.

Sadly, too often our salvation is being traded for money and fame.

The fire is close, I can literally feel the heat from hells flames as the older generation,
we are supposed to be instilling in our children, Gods Commandments an ways.

We are supposed to be lifting one another closer to Heaven with love, but too many of us stay silent when it comes to positive things to say.

Seems we would rather tear one another down thinking we'll feel better about ourselves at the end of the day. Selfishness and self-gratification is getting too much play. Morals aren't being taught, so values and self-control keeps slipping further away. Something has got to give··· It only takes one voice to provoke a change, and when two or more gather and ask for the same;

so shall it be done,
In Jesus's Mighty Name.

TONIGHT'S STORM

The thunder roared a warning
as the lightning brightened up the dark skies.

I was meditating on the sound of the rain
pounding on the ground
as the clouds
opened up wide and cried

All of a sudden my thoughts surrendered
to the negativity
like they were hypnotized

My happiness instantly
became paralyzed!!

Started wondering why nothing,
now days seems
to be going right.

Than my heart silently began to
hurt
scream
and cry.

As my sanity broke out
and strayed further and further
away from my mind.

THE SILVER LINING

It was like there was a force
somewhere out there
calling it

Magnetized

I sat and allowed the wind to blow
the rain drops in my face
so no one would notice my tear filled eyes.

All of a sudden
I found myself panicking
my chest was closing tight.

Felt like I was slowly dying inside.

My spirit begins to feel the pain
but I tried not to allow the sadness
to control my emotions this time.

Even though...
It tried!
It tried!
It tried!

I was stuck pondered on today,
meaning my present life.

THE SILVER LINING

I have been forced to turn away
exposing my other cheek
way to many times.

Engulfed in deception,
by all the surrounding betrayal and lies .

Enemies to close to me.
Posing as friends,
what a sickening disguise?

Trust
Under pressure
facing those I love

Squared up for once they decide to cross the
line.

Today I feel so alone
and where the hell is my shining knight.

Been searching all over
waiting impatiently
but he's nowhere in sight.

Give me strength Lord
I'm sick of the devils attacks
as I try focusing on this climb.

THE SILVER LINING

I know he's a thief
but will he ever stop
trying to claim what's rightfully mine.

I'm looking forward
to the morning hours hoping!
And my faith is somewhat relying

On the positive energy
released from tomorrows sunlight.

Because
TONIGHT'S STORM
has drained
what was left, even though...
I tried.

BACK 2 BASICS

I know that I need to get back to basics. A child that stays dependent on God's love.

I need to lay my worldly ways down, and allow my actions to reflect more self-control. Honestly I admit there have been plenty of times I've ignored the calls to suit up and play my role.

My heart's desires keep blocking my transformation, as it is trying to unfold, and until I align myself with His vision for me, SPIRITUALLY; I'll never grow.

I can't ignore it anymore. My heart was beginning to turn ice cold. Now, I can literally feel the Holy Spirit tugging on my soul, and the same ole same ole, eventually gets old, especially when the outcome is already very well known.

We live, but how many times is it going to take for us to learn? If you keep playing in the fire of hell, you will continue to get burned.

Sometimes it's like we're stuck on a roller coaster and the more we try to jump off, the faster it begins to turn.

Obedience to our Father's Laws and the acknowledgement of his son is how our salvation is earned.

I need to get back to basics⋯ It is the wisdom grace and favor, for which I yearn.

THE WAYWARD SOUL
(DEFINED)

WAYWARD [wey-werd] adjective

    1: Turned or turning away from what is right or proper; willful; disobedient: a wayward son; wayward behavior···

SOUL [sōl] Noun:

    1: The spiritual or immaterial part of a human being or animal, regarded as immortal···
    2. A person's moral or emotional nature or sense of identity···

THE WAYWARD SOUL

The toughest battle we will ever face will be the ongoing battle as the devil looks for ways to eliminate any purity out of our souls.
And some of us are so mentally challenged when it comes to doing what's morally correct, despite the many times proper direction has been told.

Power belongs to no man here on earth; the power resides with the man in heaven sitting on his throne. Disappointed to watch his children never choose to do what's right, when he knows he's already let our spirit know what is wrong.

We can't serve but only one God, how many of us honestly know which side it is that we belong?

Love and peace call out to us, but then there's the trickery created by Satan, and he will never cease trying to take control. We have to face him head on. His dreams I'll never buy, still there's many that view the fiery brimstone as diamonds and gold, and once he realizes he can use you, the more you can consider your salvation as being sold.

The more you're used as a vessel to bring forth destruction and chaos, the more you will stray away from the path of Gods Holy road. Everything you used to know about the truth, now your acting like you no longer know. You are going to keep losing misusing and abusing yourself and others by refusing to surrender to the inner part of yourself that's tries to make you cautious of what it is that you sow.

NATALIE

"To thy own image be true. And since I was created in the image of God. Then Father I must be true to you".

I walk off the path to quench the thirst within me, from a stream flowing uphill. I feel the minnows nibbling at my feet, as I contemplate how the Lord must feel. Up on the path hundreds constantly pass by, I go unnoticed for I occupy only a speck in time. But my value isn't measured by what I look like to them, instead it is of what I can share with them from my mind.

For if those who travel this path with me are lost, than my purpose is yet lost too. For how could I be worthy of my Father's mercy if I fail to extend that same mercy to you. I wonder if they realize that this is the road leading to The Judgment; that if there is a purgatory, it is the days that we are currently in.

A constant war of good vs evil is tugging at each of us, encouraging us to love one another as the other promotes us to sin...

Death occurred long before our birth, long before any of us ever exist. Death happened at the biting of the apple, before God wrote man's punishments onto a list.

A sense of right and wrong was unlocked when the apple was bitten; leaving us responsible for our own actions. In the end how we live is still our choice, regardless of satan's meaningless distractions...

Jesus paid a price for us a chance to get right with God, when his blood was shed on the cross... Now we all must seek to do right for the Father, by trying to guide those of us that are lost.

I watch as my enemies coax me, with adolescent trivial games. I continue to walk the path laid for me, for my purpose has not changed. His eyes tell me he is just confused, engaged in his own battle of right and wrong. Not understanding his death has already occurred, and wasting a chance to show our Father that Paradise is where we belong.

Think carefully wayward soul, earthly confrontations are just a facade. You seek to be blessed with earthly crowns, jewels and thrones, while I seek to get right with God.

I seek not to share damnation with those who chose to stray. For you, I can only distance myself, and remember you when I pray.

For these things, we fight for so passionately: {possessions, labels, egos and respect}. Those are merely the things the devil sees you covet, that he uses so that it's God you'll neglect.

I climb back up the hill and watch people cherishing their possessions, unaware that those possession will be left behind. God cares not what values you have accumulated, only that it was Him that you chose to find.

Stay steadfast in your quest to be found worthy of the Kingdom; Look for the Lord to guide us as The Judgment unfolds.

Beware of those who create turmoil and chaos, for damnation is the destination of the "Wayward Soul".

BERNARD

*LESS AND LESS *

My heart is open to any encouragement
You all can keep the rest
I want to surround myself with those
who can encourage
ME TO STAY BLESSED

My soul has reached a point
where it will no longer allow me to half step
I'm leaving the spirit of hate behind me
and searching for my spirit to be fed
Heavenly caressed
I hear no evil

My ears have now become deaf
I'll be damned if I keep allowing myself to
be put
in a place to clean up another man's mess
Please
don't take my changes personal

This is just ME
trying to pass MY PERSONAL test

THE SILVER LINING

Had to release the drama
of carrying around everyone else's stress
Still, Who gave any man the authority to
judge the way I step
Opinions are just that
I don't allow them to define me anymore or
keep me from getting any rest
I fear no man but God
So I pay no attention to all the worldly
threats
PROTECTED
Because, I keep the breastplate of
righteousness
strapped upon my chest
And it seems the more I walk towards the
light
I care about what I left in the darkness
LESS AND LESS.

*TODAY'S PRAYER *

Lord, I ask that you keep us all
grounded and sustained,
Because the devil has been busy
targeting our thoughts every day.
I know to call on you,
It is your authority
that will instantly breaks hells chains.
Lord I know your still working with us,
So as long as we repent and try to do
right,
you are still willing to forgive us for
everything.
And I pray
You continually guide us through the
wicked ways
of this world as we know it today.
Lord, signs are everywhere,
It is not the same.
The end is coming much sooner than we
think

And all of our sins combined will be to
blame.
Lord, please have mercy on those of us
who are faithful at trying to obey your
ways.
We might slide back,
but you seem to always bring us back
to our rightful place.
We love and praise your Holy name.
Thank you for blessing us with your
favor and grace.
This is my prayer for today.
I'm thanking you in advance Father,
In Jesus mighty name. Amen!

AMEN

WILLING TO FIGHT

I couldn't imagine living day to day
always focusing on negativity.
Not to say I don't ever get discouraged,
but depression will never
be allowed to take control of me.
I've been at breaking points plenty of times.
I won't even lie
Painful memories used to replay over and
over in my mind.

I couldn't see my blessings through the
heavy rains
even though there was plenty,
because I had allowed my troubles to keep
me blind.
All it took was me asking God to come back
into my life.
Instantly all of my worries were left behind.

THE SILVER LINING

Not close enough to hurt me anymore,
but not so far gone that the lessons learned
weren't still there to remind.

Thank you Lord, for being so forgiving
patient, loving, and kind.
People are still going to sleep
every night
mad, upset and crying.
I don't understand why.

Wanting to give up
feeling like their soul is already begun dying.
Although it's until our final breath
we should be,
WILLING TO FIGHT!!!

REALITY CHECK

There's no such thing as a perfect life,
and look how many of us
are still here and survived.
We really have to watch every word
we speak over ourselves
because our tongue can either welcome blessings
or bring curses into our lives.
Satan is the father of all deceit,
mind games, and lies.
There's no need to keep looking down
on yourself for your mistakes,
Look up towards heaven,
ask forgiveness, and praise the most high.
Up above,
Our Father waits on us to come
lay our burdens down,
allowing him to walk with us back into the light.
We were not created to be defeated by beast of hell,
but God will let him test us,
to see how we react to
what's wrong and what's right.
We might fail a thousand times in life,
but it's up to us to jump back into reality
and keep moving even if it's a bumpy ride.

THE SILVER LINING

THAT'S A FACT

I woke up blessed
to have yet another chance
The angels harps
are playing songs of praise,
keeping me peaceful
and in a heavenly trance.
I am focused on the future
but I'll never forget
the lessons learned from my past.
The devil is steadily calling me out,
he wants to dance.
I keep refusing to two step, to his beat.
Still, every time I turn around he's
riding my back.
It's been like a high speed chase in the
fast lane lately,
so my foots been heavy on the gas.
Everything isn't always
what it seems to be
and we end up feeling
like the spirit of failure
has us trapped.

Not me!
I know he is a liar and a thief,
and the same temptations he used to
tempt me with
can no longer do that.
With my faith, I know the Lord will
multiply
what is lost, and bring it back x three.
and THAT'S A FACT!

BEAUTY IS

So many people are too caught up
In society's big hype
of what's acceptable
And what looks wrong and right.
Beauty shouldn't be measured by
just a pretty face
slender weight or size.
My opinion
Real beauty stems from
the characteristics
That resides inside.
That beauty is what will reflect
A natural shine.
Making love easy to find.
Do you reflect peace and love?
Or is all the world gets from you
Is your negative side?
Super model status,
but how annoying is it
to hear her talk about
Herself all the time?
A hungry man on the corner asked
for a few bucks to eat
and daily gets denied.
If it was you in their shoes,
imagine how it feels to just watch
everyone walk right on right by.

Beauty to me is unselfishness
and being able to make
someone else smile.
Beauty to me is
setting your needs aside
To help a friend out for a while.
We treat the media's opinion of what
we should be,
as if it's our blueprint to the
happily ever after life.
But the truth is
we were already made uniquely
Beautiful in our creators mind.

NO DOUBT

A friend asked,
how do you know when you have truly been
forgiven.
It's a simple answer,
but remember,
this is solely based off my opinion.
There will be NO DOUBT
once you surrender to Jesus and confess,
For you will be touched
with a spiritual healing.
You'll know when your heart is no longer
weighed down
by guilt ridden feelings.
Your conscious doesn't have the leverage
to taunt you with thoughts of your past
after God lifts them out of your spirit.
He sacrificed his blood
to prove the unconditional love
He holds for all of His children.
The price has been paid
Our paths have been paved,.
We just have to follow his footsteps
and listen.

JUDGMENT DAY

Say today was judgment day.
Time is up,

you've executed the years you were allowed
here on earth for work and play.
How many of us are really aware,

Have a preference
or are even concerned with our eternal fate?

One day we will be held accountable
for every decision we have ever made.

Still, by his blood
we are not eternally bound by our mistakes.

For those that never surrendered to the truth
of the Father and asked for forgiveness,
Hell awaits.

Perfection doesn't exist here on earth,
but all you have to do is believe in his name,
and he will be there to greet you in the end,
with open arms at heavens pearly gates.

*PREDESTINED STEPS *

The victory is never really ours.

We have to remain humble
or all blessings will cease.

Having too much pride,
in the devils eyes
makes you a target
to be easily deceived.

All glory should go to the Father,
for all that's accomplished
is only done by him through me.

My gift is undeniable,
and no man can take
what the Lord has given to me.

I am only the vessel
he filled with his love,
wisdom and the courage
to spread the truth and water his seeds.

A new way.
A new reason to smile.
A new vision for tomorrow.
for all that are willing
to open their minds and believe.

THE SILVER LINING

He sits on his mighty throne waiting for those
that have strayed so far
they're scared to come and seek.

He holds the answers
that can set all of us free.

Truth is
right now were all stuck deep
in the belly of the beast.

Let us call on Jesus,
because he holds forgiveness
for when we slide back,
and has the power
to bring back the peace.

We walk the journey of our lives
but our steps
like a blueprint
are already laid.

Sad how some feel to guilty
to go back to him
and Satan
keeps 'em bound and down
by their shame
And some will continue to fail
because they were
unwilling to glorify his Holy name.

PUSHING POSITIVITY

The peace in my life
has Increased and consumed me.
Now that I see positive actions have set me free.
Burdens lifted once
all the negativity was fully released.
I didn't run to the Lord out of fear
I turned to him for love,
when I felt the rest the world was hating me.
For he is where I find my strength,
He is rock, my true refugee.
If I lead by example, all can find this same
happiness.
Well, that's what I want to believe.
God knows we are not perfect,
so we will occasionally fall victim to the enemy.
But we cannot judge one another
for what we may think,
because the only judge has already forgiven
thee.
Jesus walked the earth to spread love,
and teach us the way that we need to be.
We need to find compassion
and understanding for one another,
and learn to think before we speak.
No matter how many stones one may throw,
If you know you're doing the best you can,
continue practicing what it is that you preach
So here I stand
faithfully Pushing Positivity.

WHERE IS THE LOVE??

We were all created with love,
so WE ARE the answer
to where the love has gone.

Let us refocus,
compassion,
understanding and forgiveness
is where we all need to begin...

Emotions and grudges
control our behaviors.
Look how some people go years
without speaking to their own kin

Respect for one another has been
overlooked far too long,
We need to reestablish
that characteristic again.
The battle is not ours.
It's spiritual.

THE SILVER LINING

Good vs evil
and Gods children need to stick together
if we are going to win.

Right now the human race is losing,

Our minds not aligned with the truth
so we are bound by all of our sins.

Selfishness rules this world.

Money, and material things are desired,
yet we ignore those that don't even know
when they will eat again.

Like Cain and Able.
jealousy also plays a big role.
We just need to learn to be happy
within their own skin.
The love will start to overflow
once all of the petty hating on one
another ends.

Walls are built for protection,
but it only takes a little love to help a
broken heart to mend.

So where is the love??
Its WITHIN US
We just have to open our hearts
and let it in.

ALL OF OUR STRENGTH

Paralyzed by the past,
Scared of the future,
but she's ready
to open her heart and be freed.

Like a bird, caged,
It's been years since she's been released.
Realizing we can't let life live us,
we have to live and learn,
and forgiveness is the key.
This includes your mistakes
and all of your enemies.
Truth is, most the time
things won't always turn out
to be as it seemed.

Shouldn't be used as a crutch
or an excuse to just give up on everything.
There's signs for a conscious mind,
Lessons for self-correction
and a reminder of who and what not to be.

To many people rather
follow the next man's dreams,
even if they don't share the same beliefs.
That's why like a bird I rather fly solo,
there's no limits as far as I can see.

I know God heals all,
because many times
He's repaired my broken wings.

Our dreams are only turned into reality
with the courage to wake up and reach.
Determination for a better day
has to motivate you to soar above
the darkness that lies deep.

Fear is not an option
because faith is in the fact
that the Lord will supply all of our strength.

THE SILVER LINING

HUMANITY'S WAR

One way is their mission
but it's in the wrong direction.
We are under attack daily,
being deceived and losing to our own nation.

Spirits of darkness surround us
cloaked with a lights of hope
convincing the good
to conduct satanic business.

Keeping us focused on
what they want us to know,
but at the same time,
rubbing the truth all in our faces.

Souls traded for a name,
innocent blood sacrificed to the game.
Awareness is vital
before it's too late to spark a change.

Satan is a liar,
but the truth to those
who are desperately looking to gain.

What happened to success
being measured by the true talents you
display?
How do those who surrender
expect any real stability to remain?

THE LORD IS OUR ROCK,
OUR FOUNDATION!

It was pure greed,
that provoked them to stray

Who's looking ahead to see
everything we're living for now,
in the end
won't mean a thing.
Except total destruction
for the whole human race.

How long will our loving father allow them
to defile his ways and his Holy name?
They'll be bound to the fire
after the chosen are lifted to enter heaven's
pearly gates.

Smoke
and ashes over dirt will be the world's only
remains.
This is serious
Lives
Rights
and freedom of speech
are slowly being ripped away.

We were warned the devil would gain
control,
this is our final test.
Will we condone the evil one
by putting Gods Laws to rest?

Knowledge of this situation
is the way to keep your mind safe.
Stay prayed up
Protected
And blessed.

BORN TO BE FREE

Like a dove
I want to be able to fly free.

As high as the clouds,
where no one can see.

Just me and my lover
cruising the skies
in perfect sync.

Singing love songs
as we sit at the top
of the highest tree.

No concerns,
No need to worry
what the next day may bring.

Living in the moment only
enjoying the blossoming beauty
of nature's natural seeds.

Crisp green grass
and colorful flowers begin to grow
as the sun and rain
supplies all their needs.

THE SILVER LINING

As I enjoy the scents
the morning breezes bring,
I dance and rejoice
through the cool morning mist
that falls and covers everything.

Traffic jams
causing interesting commotion,
as big people constantly flood the
streets.

Children playing
and laughing carelessly,
until the school bells finally rings.

I rely on no one,
and give praises to my creator
for my life is full
of plenty blessings.

When I feel too weak,
I go to him
and he replenishes
all of my strength.

It is a smile on his face
that I seek.

THE SILVER LINING

For
he never expected
me to be anyone but me.

So I soar
fully extended wings

Just living my life
I was BORN TO BE FREE.

THE CARETAKER

Like a thief in the night,
The Caretaker works collecting souls of those ready
to eternally close their eyes.
The fallen soldiers of the streets,
or the elderly
who have finally lost the will to survive.

The sick,
sometimes they just give up,
seemed as if they were only living
to fight for their lives.
Who really wants to keep suffering just to stay alive?
The innocent children,
that are being beaten
and mistreated,
sometimes to the point of death.

Which are the most important
for him to keep close to him,
for there is still so much innocence left.

Unlike The Grim Reaper
who comes surrounded by darkness
he walks out of the light to greet them
the moment they take their final breath.

THE SILVER LINING

Only empty vessels lay behind

Left to return from which they were made.
His only job is to guide them back home.

Safely where they belong

The Lord sighs and smiles.

His child has returned
and the angels surround the reunion dancing
and singing praises through music and songs.

The Lord embraces his child and says
For you, our separation felt like centuries
but in my time you weren't gone very long.

It seems like only yesterday
I pre-wrote your journey and sent you on your way.
Yes, countless mistakes were made
but I continued loving you despite of it all.

Forgiveness was my gift to you since the day
I surrendered myself to the cross.
Admit it my child
I was there for you every time you called.

The caretaker came to you
because I sent him to ensure that your soul
wasn't lost.

THE SILVER LINING

MY REFLECTIONS

MIRROR MIRROR ON THE WALL.
THE WORLD
VIEWS ME AS BEING STRONG.
NOT TO SAY
THEIR JUDGMENTS WRONG.
IT'S JUST WHEN I LOOK
UPON MY OWN REFLECTION,
I SEE THE WHOLE JOURNEY
FROM WHICH I HAVE COME FROM.

At times I have disconnected.

Even I have felt neglected and rejected.

If you only knew how it's always been me against
the world.

I give
and I gave
My everything at all times,
yet...
nothing ever seemed to be returned.
My life screwed me over
and left me all alone.
Robbing the innocence of what
used to be a sweet little girl.

THE SILVER LINING

I started to lose my mind,
losing the fight for my life
Until I opened the door up for the Lord.

He sparked a change,
showed me the right path,
dried my tears
and erased all of my pain.

Taught me how to forgive all those
from my past that I blamed.

My father is worthy of all the praise.

He was the treasure I discovered.
Far much greater than a four leaved clover.

So I decided to turn a new leaf over.
I was tired of getting burned,
I couldn't just keep standing there
feeling sorry for myself as the world
around me continued to turn.

Instead of looking beyond with fear
I approached and conquered it all
with the lessons that I have learned.

Now I fear nothing because even if I lose
I know tomorrow I'll have another turn.

THE SILVER LINING

MIRROR MIRROR ON THE WALL.
THE WORLD VIEWS ME AS BEING STRONG.
NOT TO SAY THEIR JUDGMENTS WRONG.
IT'S JUST WHEN I LOOK UPON MY OWN
REFLECTION,
I SEE THE WHOLE JOURNEY
FROM WHICH I HAVE COME FROM.

I KNOW OF A PLACE

I know of a place
Where angels harmonize by rubbing
wings.
And all around you is filled with
beautiful things.

Where pain nor sorrow
Will ever exist.
This place is special,
For there's no other like this.
This place doesn't have concrete,
For you walk on clouds.
And there's plenty of room,
So there is no crowds.

You never want for anything,
For all is right there.
And when you hear I love you,
You know they care.
A place where God's love is felt,
Every moment of everyday.
And the sun shines bright,

THE SILVER LINING

As it does in May.
A place were a kid has nothing to worry
about,
Except for being a kid.
A place where God will bless you,
For all that you have did
No more needing help to stand,
Or having to watch what you eat.

Or hearing about a teenager,
Who died in the streets
Where your body has no form
Because it was only a shell.

But you live on
For your spirit is where you truly dwell.
I know you're now dancing
Like you haven't for years.
And you know we'll miss you
That's why we're shedding these tears.
Gone but not forgotten,
Because the lessons you've taught live on.
But still can't help but hurt,
Because now you are gone.

I know when I make it,
I'll find you there between the Father
and Son.
Because they only called you home,
Because your job on earth was well done.
Until the day I see you again,
There's still much I have to do.

But I doubt a day will go by,
When I don't think of you.

I love you mama R.I.P.

Dedicated to my mother
~Barbara Jean Whitaker~

THE SILVER LINING

"*PICKED FROM THE GARDEN*"
(WITH BERNARD WASHINGTON)

If the children are our future,
we need to pay better attention.
Instead of doing all the talking,
slow down and just listen.

Cause Satan's on a mission,
to win at any cost.
And he takes pride in his work,
Every time another child is lost.

Have we ever really learned
from what we went through with Columbine?
Are we ignoring warning signs;
or are we really that blind.

Kids are killing kids,
at a rate that's alarming.
Precious roses being plucked,
From within the midst of the garden.

Kids look to us for guidance,
cause elders are supposed to be wise.

But we fail to detect the changes in their lives,
which we need to understand are their silent cries.

~BERNARD~

THE SILVER LINING

Where are the answers
to help us mend this broken world.
Truth is there isn't any because to many are clueless
as to what's really going on.

There are children in the room next to where their
parents are resting planning to kill,
and learning how to make bombs.

Communication with our children
is the only place a true understanding
of what they are going through
will ever come from.

Now days most parents don't take the time to find
out where their kids are safe,
or don't find the time
to simply protect them from harm.

Apparently
they felt like they couldn't talk to anyone,
now their roaming around with loaded guns.

Just like the weather though,
there's always signs to predict
when a storm is going to come.

As parents we have to make ourselves available,
a shelter to which they can run.
If you refuse to correct them, you're just as much to
blame when something goes terribly wrong.

~ NATALIE ~

THE SILVER LINING

Kids busting caps outta guns,
instead of busting out caps and gown.
No more running for the bell,
now they running from the popping sound.

Because they've been embarrassed,
or ostracized.
Feeling like they don't fit in,
but nobody realize.

A child that's lost,
but it seems the world doesn't care.
And the parents can't help,
cause many aren't even there.

Then people want to scream,
and pray to God
for the kids after it's too late.
Why can schools teach them about Hitler,
But can't mention God
cause of "Church vs. State.

We're failing our kids,
and the devil doesn't give out pardons.
Only God can lead us through this,
and prevent another rose from being
"Picked from The Garden"

~BERNARD~

THE SILVER LINING

GENERATIONS

(WITH BERNARD WASHINGTON & DAIMIAN E)

Hey Brotha,
Can I have a few words.
I want to know why,
They packing your generation in the penitentiary like
herds.

Can't you see that it's all,
A new form of slavery.
That the street life now,
Isn't a sign of bravery.

Back in my days,
It meant having responsibilities to be considered a
man..
And we settled shit with our fist,
Not with a gun in hand.

Now days,
Ya'll don't show no kind of respect.
Bring a kid in this world,
Only to teach them neglect.

This worlds fucked up,
And the blame lies on you.
Cause when it comes to bringing a change,
Your generation haven't the slightest clue.

~ *BERNARD WASHINGTON* ~

[69]

THE SILVER LINING

Ha I laugh at remarks like that. They throwing my generation in the Penitentiary because of ya'll sins, Because of your generation young black men like me are guilty until proven innocent because of the color of our skin.

First of all my generation Isn't in the streets to be brave, Our fathers left us with single mothers, So it's up to us to grind hard to help put food on the table and make sure the bill's get paid.

I guess your generation must've forgot Or no longer care to understand, You talk about settling problems with your fist, Well back in the day's The Black Panther's use to walk around with automatic weapons in their hand's.

Either you naive or your history isn't caught up, because before I was even born your generation created gangs for young men like me to be a part of.

I the elder's should practice what they preach, because my father was a part of your generation and he left my mother a single black woman to raise me.

Please listen this world was fucked up and corrupted before I even existed. Your generation is quick to preach but hesitate to teach.

How do you expect us to make a change, When your generation isn't standing up to do the same. We haven't the slightest clue because it isn't a mystery, that some of the faults of my generation being fucked up, Rest's in your generation history.

~ DAIMIAN E. ~

[70]

THE SILVER LINING

Generation to generation,
Yes, some things will be passed on
and some will change.

We will all be held accountable individually
for our own mistakes.

Although, I do agree and believe those prior years is
what set the tone for today.

It's irrelevant who's guilty of what though,
for different reasons maybe, but we are all to blame.

Truth is the transformations
of the new breeds begin at home.

They can only blossom from the seeds
of life from which they were s(h)own.

What is the good life?
Reality is there is too many broken homes.

Single parent families working over 40 hours a week,
so the kids are raising their selves alone.

That's where all the love and discipline
of our youth has gone.

If guidance and direction is
going to be overlooked at home,
you better known society will surely steer them wrong.

Violence has been around since the beginning
and the numbers continue
to keep growing strong.

THE SILVER LINING

The level of respect that we have for one another is
what really causes the problem.

Instead of fighting heads up, It seems 2 legit to use
guns and knives to solve them.

Instead of all the finger pointing and arguing, lets unite,
maybe together we'll finally get it right.

We are not enemies,
the human race vs. Satan is the real fight.

From the beginning to the end of time, Jesus has, and
will be the source of every
Generation's light.

~ NATALIE DIXON ~

THE SILVER LINING

SAY WHAT YOU MEAN, MEAN WHAT YOU SAY

We have to learn to be quick to listen
and slow to speak.

Sometimes,

we make ourselves appear foolish
expressing what we THINK

Why's it so hard for people
to just say what they really mean,

and mean what they say?

To many claiming to be real,
but their actions
prove them to be nothing but a fake.

If you can't embrace
and express your own truth,
most likely something
has you feeling ashamed.

THE SILVER LINING

Face the truth and ask forgiveness,
otherwise,
you'll continue to be a waste
of someone else's time.

Hearts usually are affected by the
confusion
of another one's mind.

Covering up one lie with another
doesn't make the truth go away.

You only keep suppressing truths pain.

You can bury your secrets
as deep as you want,
but they will expose their self-one day

You owe It to yourself and others,
to say what you mean and
mean what you say

Life is a struggle of its own,
no one has time to keep playing games.

THAT LITTLE GIRL

I wonder if my mother ever imagined
"THAT LITTLE GIRL"
she was raising would blossom
into the wonderful woman
I am today.

Strong willed
the motivation to build,
and humble enough to still appreciate .

Sometimes even I look back in amazement
at all the mountains of troubles
I have overcome.

Fatherless,
Ma's constantly struggling,
I've been abused ,
and I'm a survivor of rape.

I had to take on the role of a
fighter at an early age.

The things I seen the women
in my family go through
made me really
focus on what not to take.

THE SILVER LINING

I took notes on how to never behave,
and to stay real to myself.
Even if I happened to be surrounded
with nothing but fake

unlike the usual
that fall into all of their families
dysfunctional ways.

I'm not a scholar with top grades,

But I have been schooled,
So you can say that I'm "self-made".

What I know from experience,
I share it,
in hopes of helping the next woman
that may be going through the same.

Not to mention,
you really can't claim to know someone
unless you know from where they have come.

The cream will always rise to the top,
you just have to let the pot simmer,
be patient, and wait.

THE SILVER LINING

Wisdom didn't come naturally,
I admit...
I'm also a woman of so many mistakes.

But they won't continue to hold me down,
I been soaring since I gave,
and the Lord took all my burdens away.

I know when I close my eyes at night
I'm waking up to a new start,
another chance to progress and change.

Mama I know you have to be proud of me
and all that I've accomplished.
You're probably looking down from heaven
with the biggest smile on your face.

LIVE AND LEARN

First it's going to hurt,
but after the pain,
understanding will set in.

Just like after
being burned one time,
were not so quick
to play with fire again.

Take life for what it is worth,
instead of allowing the past
to justify who you are today.

We have got to learn to not
pack so much baggage
when we walk away.

I know there's been
stormy weather surrounding you
but don't you see
how bright the sun is
shining today?

Here it is to dry away the tears
the world cried on us yesterday.
We have to work hard for what we want,

[78]

THE SILVER LINING

Get use to it,
there is no easy way.
Keep thinking there is
and you will continue to
get yourself played.

We have to reach further
to catch our dreams
before we let them
get too far away.

That's when we end up
settling for less
just trying to fill up
any empty space.

How can you ever win
if you're too scared to
even play the game
Practice is needed
in order to win
so don't let a few losses
scare you from trying again.

If you don't think
you deserve better
than you can't complain
when you find yourself
in that same place again.

SELF DESTRUCTION

Without unity and organization,
we'll continue to destroy ourselves,
bringing continued shame
to the human name
and every race.
For every negative action
there is a positive we will have to pay.
Let's learn to encourage ourselves
and make new goals every day.
Love is the light,
through all the darkness
we can lead one another
in the right way.
Leaving no 1 behind
having the compassion to
help those that have strayed.
We are all family through our creator,
so how can we continue to act helpless
as our brother is slayed?
LORD , have mercy on us
this world has went into a complete rage.
Blood continually shed,
with hopes of power an fame being gained.
Where's the peace on this earth,
things are not the same.
my eyes are focused on heaven,
but underneath I'm starting to feel
the heat from hells' flames!!!

LOVE, COMPASSION, AND FORGIVENESS

When you're in love with someone
you're willing to overlook certain traits
you personally don't like.

Think about it,
we receive that same kind of love
from Jesus Christ..

So why are we so quick to Judge,
Blame and hate one another,
knowing that characteristics
within ourselves isn't right

God expects us
to be more compassionate
to one another,
by trying to see their past
through our own eyes.
It's easier to forgive someone

If you take the time to understand
what went on in their life

THE SILVER LINING

Some of us had to grow up to fast

Some of us always came in last

Some of us had our innocence snatched

Some of us grew up with
everything handed to them

So they really don't understand
the life or thoughts of the struggling man.

We could break all the misunderstandings

Finding a way to love one another

if we will be more like Jesus
and react to the world with more compassion.

We have to stop letting our quest
for things of the world
to determine our reactions.

it's only through JESUS CHRIST
we can, as a whole,
find true satisfaction.

THE STORM CHASERS

The wind increases its speed
Shaking every single branch on the tree.

All the leaves take the same beating,
but only the weak ones tend to
break off and fall beneath .

That's only the warning of what's yet to
come,
suddenly clouds consume the light,
and the skies begin to speak.

Thunder roars through the lands,
As the lightning produces
flashes of deathly streaks.

So much power,
one strike and the force behind it,
could destroy anything.

Most people would run and take cover,
but then there's those that,
thrive and live for chasing troubles.

THE SILVER LINING

Instead of searching for higher grounds,
they feel more comfortable
being tossed below amongst all the rubble...

I call them the storm chasers.
They really don't want to see
beyond the rainy days...

Subconsciously they're probably hoping,
one of the storms would
just sweep them away.

Secretly wishing for death,
and underestimating mother nature's wrath,
is like playing suicide games.

Nothing positive comes to them,
because all their negativity controls
and binds their faith.

They're something like that black cloud that
releases the storms heaviest rains.

JESUS' TAKE THE LEAD

Jesus take the lead.

I cannot do it on my own
I need your guidance please

I admit at times I walk through the
darkness,
but every time you are there to re light
the way for me.

I'll forever praise your name father,
for you continue to forgive every time
you hear my pleas.

You know I am not perfect
You are the only one,
and without you
the whole human race will stay weak.

If we call on you

You'll come running.
there's been plenty of times you have
already proved that to me.

THE SILVER LINING

It's my fault
if I don't turn my life over to you
Giving you full control
that's why I am here today,
asking that you to take the lead.

Every step I take
Every move I make
I want to look beside me and see the
footprints of your feet.
Not only will you keep me
on the right path,
but I know you can carry me through,
further than the human eye can see.

*Natalie *

I've tried to walk this journey,
through the valley of the Shadows of
Death.

Often times my decisions,
have left me with no options left.

For it seems that my best thinking,
has led to my own demise.

THE SILVER LINING

So I fall to my knees,
and ask the Lord to open my eyes.

Father take my hand,
each time I begin to stray.

For I intend not,
to be defiant,
I simply sometimes lose my way.

I call out your name Lord,
please guide your child back to the
light.

For I know that your love for us,
will make everything alright.

That's why that day on Calvary,
to give us a second chance you chose to
bleed.

And the only way to Our Father is
through you.
So please,

"Jesus Take The Lead"

* Bernard Washington*

TRICK OR TREAT

Why is it every time the Lord
tries to bless us with a treat,
the Devils at work overtime
with a list full of tricks?

He stays on a mission

The thief of the night
comes to steal,
kill,
and destroy ,
GODS eternal gifts.

Hold on tight

Because he's going show up
every single time
and do his best to make us loose our grip.

Not wanting us to enjoy the benefits of
anything that's been heaven sent.

He hopes we'll sign our souls to him
so he can add our name on the chambers of
hells' list.

THE SILVER LINING

We have to stand firmly on our faith

because without it,
our whole mental will be invaded
day by day until we give up and flip.

We cannot surrender to depression,
lost hope,
or any unhappiness.

That is not the life our loving
Father intended on us to live.

If we live by his standards,
walk his walk,
there's no limit to the blessings he'll give.

Why is it so easy
to treasure things of the world

but we think twice
when it comes to honoring
JESUS,
and he was our most sufficient gift.

To give us security and offer a new way
to the Holy land is why he was sent.

We were never expected to be perfect

It's his blood on that cross that
cleanses all of our sins.

HIS CREATION

I'll continue to keep my eyes
focused on heaven,
For the Lord is my
only help and salvation .

HE MAY PUNISH US,
BUT HE WOULD NEVER TURN HIS
BACK ON US

HIS CREATION.

We may reap what we sow,
it has been written.
So why do we want to turn
the blame on him
when our past comes back to take control.

Instead of holding grudges
against the Lord,
Look towards heaven,
surrender your love.
and he will help you
carry the load.

NO GUARANTEES

The next day is never been promised,
we have to learn to live for today.

Knowing the TRUTH,

My outlook on life on earth
and death has changed.

Our Earthly bodies are not forever

Heaven is our home
for The eternal stay.

These days here are only TEST,

given to us to learn
how to make our way.

Will we surrender to him
and walk the paths FOR US he has laid.

Or will we submit to the devil's plots ,
and worship material things and worldly
ways..

Failing to give

The ALMIGHTY HIS LOVE AND PRAISE.

Are we ALL EVEN worthy,

for all the wonders above God has
previously tucked away.

When trouble hits us

do we worry as our faith
In his love slip away.

I call on JESUS

He'll always honor
EVERY promises he's made.

Sometimes we may think he has strayed

But he answers our prayers on his own time,
yet he is never late.

JUST WAIT

Everyone waits their whole life
for the one that will make
their soul feel complete.

But we get impatient
waiting for the chosen one
that God intends to send our way.

Patience reveals real love,
as frustrated as we may get,
sometimes we just have to wait.

For most of us
it wares down on us emotionally,

So we rush into relationships
hoping for the wrong person
to come and fill the void of that empty space.

Which usually doesn't take long
for our actions to backfire
right in our face.

While we're wrapped up
in trying to choose our own fate.

THE SILVER LINING

Our blessing has come and gone,

so now we want to question GOD
to why your soul is stuck
in this lonely state.

Not realizing,
we chose our own path,
so it's our own mistake.

JUST WAIT!

STRONGER THAN EVER

I feel stronger than ever.
Daily I face this world alone.
Times get hard but without thinking,
I know I always have to
just keep pushing on.
No time to feel bad for myself,
There's not always going to be a
justified reason
for all the drama
that continues to go on.
Seems like I can take 2 steps ahead,
and a twist a fate takes me right back
where I started from.
No time to feel sorry for myself,
Been stuck there
and done for far too long.
I have found my independence now,
and since then, through it all,
I remain focused and standing strong.
I've learned not to depend
on anyone but myself,
and with the Lord is where all of my
faith belongs!!!

THE BROKEN SOUL

So lonely and afraid,
she's been a loner since back in the day.
She lets no one get to close,
for she has experienced years full of pain.
She's realizing now,
keeping to herself doesn't help the burden
of the past go away.
So depressed,
She just cries herself to sleep each night as she lays.
A miracle
A blessing
A change for better is what she awaits.
A reason to finally live,
laugh,
and smile every waking day.
I tell her, all you have to do is surrender,
Get on your knees and pray.
He is the keeper of our soul,
so when It's broken
It's only because we have somehow strayed.
Go to him now,
and thank him for the sacrifices
for your life he previously made.
Express to him how your sorry
for every single mistake.
Ask him to take your heart,
Cleanse it,
and make it brand new today.

There's no way we can fail
if we read his word and follow his ways.
There's no way he wants to see his creation
filled with heartache,
Confusion,
or pain.
But you have to be the one
to reach out and call on his name.
Of course times are hard,
We have to learn to stop letting Satan always have
his way.
Take some authority
and tell him to get out of your way.
Send him right back to hell in Jesus' name.

HEAVEN IS MY FATE

I closed my eyes
and allowed my mind to freely soar.
I found myself knock
knock
Knocking on heaven's door.
A tour of the blessed land
is what i was in store for.
Remain faithful daughter,
and you will soon earn your wings.
Eternal laughter and love is promised,
as soon as you prove worthy to pass these
gates.
He told me how he did his part to ensure
he'll be seeing my face.
He's sure for he instilled me with
wisdom,
Love,
and grace.
Reminded me how he laid his life
down,
so no sin would ever stand in my way.

THE SILVER LINING

He agreed, life here seems like hell,
but heaven is my fate.
I quickly dropped to my knees
and cried out to be released from these
heavy chains .
I get caught up sometimes Father and I
lose my faith.
"I knew no one would be perfect my little
angel", he said,
So please don't feel ashamed.
Call on me for forgiveness daily
and repent is what he explained.
He already knew with his children
living in this world,
perfection would be hard to maintain..

FINAL DESTINATION

We was all born to die,
and the ability 2 smile through happy times.

The ability to cleanse the pain we may feel
through the tears we cry.

Living in this world was never meant to be easy,
because this is only
a temporary place that our soul resides.

But not so hard, that we can't make it,
our strength comes from the most high.

Just ask,
He carries a never ending supply.

It's our choice,
follow GODS' truths to find the open door and walk
within his light,
or stay in the darkness
by believing all of Satan's paralyzing lies.

Chose to stand up,
dust yourself off and continue to rise.

It's a learning process,
so don't be discouraged
even if you fail and fall 100 times.

THE SILVER LINING

I've embraced the survivor inside of me,
because I'll be damned if I will ever play the role of
the victimized.

The promises have been made,
the boundaries for heaven or hell have been paved.

Today we face hell on earth,
but my faith keeps me focused knowing I'm worthy
for all the eternal treasures on the flip side.

My final destination point, is HEAVEN,
To watch the angels rejoice our homecoming,
as I stand by our fathers side.

FOOTPRINTS IN THE SAND

Lord, I am putting my life in your hands,
and I praise you
for allowing me yet ANOTHER chance.
my past is just that!
I know now
there's no need
for me to keep looking back.
I am focused on you JESUS,
but I have to be honest,
I get tempted when the world
is trying to pull me back.
Luckily today,
I feel your presence here,
gently whispering in my ear,
to stay on track.
"I have better things awaiting you Natalie,
but your actions have to stay aligned with my
plans".
he says " I know you have doubts,
but learn to have faith in yourself too,
for I know that you can.
I RAISED you to be strong
and to never fear no man.
He told me not to forget that it is him
that carries me through all the storms,
than he asked,
"Haven't you ever realized,
that there is only one set of
FOOTPRINTS IN THE SAND?"

FROM THE CRADLE TO THE GRAVE

From the cradle to the grave
She couldn't help but to wonder why the
love she gave
is constantly returned with hate.

She carries the world on her shoulders,
and lifts it up every time she prays.

From the cradle to the grave
A solider, still alive,
only because she keeps Gods armor and
truth in its rightful place.

Jesus came to spread love
through what he taught,
and some people
even treated him the same.

From the cradle to the grave
She lives on through all the judgments,
It's laughter that keeps her heart in a
happy state.

Confident,
so the not so confident try to bring her
to their level
by making her feel ashamed.

THE SILVER LINING

Won't happen,
she's imperfect,
but she's content with
the woman that her life has made.

From the cradle to the grave
Her spirit soars,
and her wings will be attached
as soon as she returns to the dirt
from which she came.

It seems as if a life full of battles from
the womb is what has sealed her fate.

Being a part of Gods army isn't easy,
but what's been promised in return
for her obedience
is very well worth the wait.

From the cradle to the grave
She remains humble,
although her rewards from Heaven
floods the gates.

A heart of iron beats inside of her
chest,
but the outside is as beautiful
as pearls, gold, and lace.

THE SILVER LINING

The mold was destroyed,
so she's unique in every way.

From the cradle to the grave
At the age of 3
a car wreck claimed her life,
but God sent her back to Earth.

She was needed here,
so our reunion would have to wait.

A child with no innocence left,
over and over again,
that too was taken away.

She has been constantly fighting
demons
and demon possessed spirits
to keep her joy in place ...

From the cradle to the grave
She could have been given up,
but surrendering is not an option,
she's a survivor in every way.

Targeted,
because she uplifts herself and others,
so Lucifer has always attempted to
discredit her name.

WAIT TIL YOUR FATHER COMES HOME

Although no one knows the exact time
our Father promised us all he would be back.
The separation was only temporary,
Giving us the chance to prove ourselves
worthy.
We have to be disciplined enough to avoid
the world,
stay focused,
and on track.
It just saddens my heart
for those who have once known him,
and still chose to turn their backs on the
facts.
Because I know in the end
Face to face,
they will have to own up to that.
His forgiving ways and love is never ending,
so whatever the devil has took
always know you can get it back.
Signs are everywhere
that we don't have any more time to slack.

The things that we face today
have been previously stated in Revelations,
Instead of taking heed many still ignore and

laugh.
Some rather keep giving credit for Gods
work
to science and man imagine that..
The blood he sacrificed for our salvation
was a heavy price to pay.
For those who don't respect it,
will soon feel the flames of his wrath.
And for those of us who live his word
It is our responsibility
to help all of his children to find the right
path.
The time is now, another day isn't
guaranteed,
so whatever burdens are keeping you bound,
humble yourself before Jesus Christ and let
them be set free.
Only then, will his blessings flow,
and the truth inside of you will begin to
unfold,
We lose ourselves trying to find the answers
to everything.
His plans are so complex, even if he revealed
it,
most men still wouldn't be able to
comprehend it or believe.
Why is it easy for us to put our trust in
men of the world as it is today,
yet so hard to have faith in what's unseen

although proof of his existence and love lives
inside of you and me .
NATALIE

Seed of the holy one
beat bleed and died for this sin sick world.
Pass down on me power from above.
Son of evil don't step to me
your weak get under my feet.
No place for you, get behind me
My Father business I must keep.
Hustle for souls sling scriptures,
Holy Ghost hitting them with quickness.
Spiting bible verses, giving some miracles
and to those that fight their last rites.
Hearts so cold they hate
despite the uttering of the name Jesus
Christ.
You're not the King they laugh,
heart so cold they can't break free.
Despite the fact they breath the gift of life
daily,
they're still denying the power that they
see.
With each breath they take lying to
yourself,
man didn't make the sky nor the sun or
moon.
Growing colder day by day, this world is lost.

With knowledge and power from above
keeping me strong.
So I keep this weight in my hand ready to
fire off some knowledge
for a sin sick world...
that's lost can't help but fight back tears
their my family my kin.
Damned to hell if they don't listen.
Please listen God is calling your name, won't
you listen just listen.
To rain as it plays a steady beat drip drop
drip drop.
Doesn't it make you sad; gloomy is day that
may be your last.
Wake up love ones His wrath is soon to
come.
Mama may have never told you but I will,
you don't want to not be ready when your
Father comes home.
* JESUS'S SON *

A LITTLE FAITH

Imagine having the toughest day ever,
but you didn't felt overwhelmed or
stressed.

It's possible if WE allow it,
our Father will guide us
down the right path of our personal
quests.

We hold ourselves back by living with
regrets,

because a guilty conscious will
have you comfortable with settling for
less.

Imagine the relief that you'd feel
knowing all your trials, tribulations
and mistakes were only Gods test.

THE SILVER LINING

Think of all the wasted energy we put
into
trying to clean up our own mess.

When all we had to do is hand our
problems
over to Jesus, because he can handle
them best.

Have A little Faith in his promises
whenever we call on him,
and he will show up to put all worries
chaos and confusion to rest.

O' What a wonderful feeling it is
to know Gods love, and to know what
it truly means to be blessed.

It isn't about the material things of the
world,
it's knowing our creator personally loves
you,

and the completeness you feel within.

As you learn to open you heart and soul
searching to be close to only him.

It's knowing that you are forgiven,
because God loved us so much he sent
his only son to be held accountable for
all of OUR SINS.

All his children are worthy,
and having Just A little faith is where it
all begins.

A WOMAN'S WORTH

Trying to measure a woman's worth
is as senseless as the day
Adam took the apple from Eve
despite what he was told, and still took that bite.

It's like foolishly wasting time
trying to break codes
to figure out some kind of scientific reasoning
to explain Gods complex designs.

The world tried to keep us down ,
said we belong at home bare footed and pregnant ,
they even tried to prevent us from
speaking our minds.

When the truth is it's within us women
that the answers to all the confusion is,
and has been at the whole time.

We are led by intuitions, Instincts, and signs
Which if followed will help us all survive.
By any means necessary,
we will always find the strength
to overcome our battles and rise .

Who else would God had gave the ability
to be able to nurture all of human kind,
Other than those that he trusted
and directed to be productive
and reproduce human life?

[114]

THE SILVER LINING

No man here on earth
can keep A real woman down
when she was created to soar
and given plenty of room to
fully spread wings and fly.

So why was anyone surprised
when women stood up
and united to fight
for respect and equal rights?
A woman's worth can never truly be measured,
because just like fine wine,
our value steadily increases with time.

*A WOMAN SCORNED *

She's loud mouth and rude
and always taking her problems out
on those around her every day.
In her own mind she's sincere,
but everyone around her
can see everything about her is fake.
An eye 4 an eye, Life is her battlefield
She's bitter and emotionally torn
so someone has to pay.

Alone,
and misery loves company,
so she'll trap you into her web
before she reveals the games she plays.
She lives in a world of her own
and those that enter
seem to never stay.

She came to me for answers one day
as to why I thought she keeps ending up
right back in the same lonely place
Yes, I told her,
I know you've had a rough life,
but it's no excuse
to continue behaving in such FOUL ways.

THE SILVER LINING

We as woman have all had our issues
but we have to own up
and stop trying to justify our
mistakes...

Honesty and forgiveness
will push them skeletons
in the closet out
emptying the cluttered space.

Otherwise they will keep you confused,
and living a paranoid life
thinking love
is just another word for hate.

Humble yourself and remain that way.
Only then will you invite and reflect a
true lady of grace.
In order to grow you have got to
stop allowing the past
to determine your fate.

There's no easy road
so stop wasting time looking for the
easy way.
The life handed to you
is what you need to wake up and face.

THE SILVER LINING

Start a new chapter
and say goodbye
to your old habits an ways.

Break yourself FREE
from these vicious CYCLES and CHAINS.
With GOD all things are possible!

Satan can be tamed.
Your true purpose needs to be claimed.
If you truly want to change your fate

Just Have a little faith.
Then I wiped the tears
that were flowing down her face

Held her hands in mine
looked up to the our Father
and together we prayed.

THE SILVER LINING

THE ABSENCE OF PURPOSE

"LONELINESS IS NOT THE ABSENCE OF
PEOPLE,
IT'S THE ABSENCE OF PURPOSE".

WHEN YOU FIND YOUR PURPOSE
THE NEW YOU WILL ATTRACT EVERYTHING
ELSE.

SO INSTEAD OF LOOKING FOR SOMEONE TO
MAKE YOU HAPPY,
LOOK FOR WAYS TO FIND HAPPINESS
WITHIN YOURSELF.

WE CANT HOLD ON TO THE PAST
FOREVER,
LEARN TO MAKE THE BEST OUT OF WHAT
WE'VE BEEN DEALT.

WE WERE ALL CREATED WITH A PURPOSE
AND IT LAYS DEEP WITHIN OUR HEARTS.

WE'RE NOT REALLY
LIVING OUR LIVES TO THE FULLEST

[119]

UNTIL WE SET OUR DESIRES AND WHAT
WE THINK WE NEED
TO THE SIDE AND FOCUS ON WHAT THE
LORD TRULY WANTS.

WE CONSTANTLY PRAY FOR THINGS TO
COME OUR WAY
AND GET DISCOURAGED WHEN THEY
DON'T,
BUT WE HAVE TO KNOW IT'S NOT GOING TO
EVER COME
IF IT IT'S NOT ALIGNED WITH THE GODS
THOUGHTS.

WE WERE CREATED IN HIS IMAGE
AND HE LOVED US SO MUCH,
FOR OUR FORGIVENESS
HE SURRENDERED HIMSELF TO THE
CROSS.
OUR SOULS BELONG TO HIM ETERNALLY
IT WAS WITH HIS OWN BLOOD THAT HE
PAID THE COST.
HE IS FOREVER MIGHTY,
HE IS OUR FATHER, OUR KING, THE ALPHA
BOSS.

*THE DEVIL IS A LIE *

The devil is a lie and a thief.
Here to make life hell on earth,
is what his intentions seem to be.
He is also the father of jealousy and all deceit.
Sending his demonic spirits in and out of
everybody.

He has too many of us bound.
Voicing his own opinions through each other,
causing negativity and chaos when we speak.
Where is the love, the respect and our peace.
Together that's what we as a whole need to
seek.

Our tongues can be considered as
deadly weapons,
words are more powerful than what we think.

To many rather watch the next man fall,
instead of doing right,
and helping him get back up on his feet.

Loyalty is what my veins bleed,
and the truth is what I'll continue to seek and
preach.

THE SILVER LINING

When we hurt one another, was that action
truly our own intentions?
I say no, it's the spirits that won't let us be.

We have to acknowledge the real battle,
and it's so much bigger than you and me.
So from this day on,

I'm refusing to let the devils plots keep hold of
me.

THE DEVIL IS A LIE
And I'm going to keep rebuking him until he
sets me free.

BACK ON TRACK

Because of his dedication and love for his
creation.
Knowing our future,
and that as humans we would not be perfect.
Far from it!
He put his life on the line
so we could constantly be forgiven.
He knew how rough and tempting
the world would be that we live in.
He displays a never ending love
no matter what troubles we go get ourselves in.
The message today is
whatever sins it is that we have committed.

Never, if you ask will they go unforgiven.
So don't ever use them as an excuse to not call
on him.
It was before our worldly parents existed we
were his children.
It's His breath that daily keeps us breathing.
Even though no longer dead,
Jesus allowed them to beat and kill him.
To leave a reminder that he has our back.
When we feel lost and alone
just know that's far from being a fact.
Lift your hands and reach for heaven
and you'll feel him touch you right back.

THE SILVER LINING

It's through our hearts, minds, and souls
that we are able to interact.
Some of us may feel that we've stayed away
too far to even consider turning back.
Well I'm here to say it's never too late
to reclaim the promises for us that he has laid
out.

For he already knew our flesh would be WEAK.
and if it was a promise set in stone with
conditions
I don't believe he would of surrendered
and let them stretch him out.
It was for every one of us that he allowed that
And every day he shows us signs of his
love trying to call us back
He is patiently waiting for his children to get
back on track.

www.ingramcontent.com/pod-product-compliance
Lightning Source LLC
Chambersburg PA
CBHW061737020426
42331CB00006B/1267